Total Balance Farm

Other books by the author:

NOVELS

The Member-Guest
War Memorials
The Weatherman
Haints

POETRY

Labyrinthiad
Sidetracks
Wind Over Water
Dead Languages

TOTAL BALANCE FARM

Poems

Clint McCown

Press 53
Winston-Salem

Press 53, LLC
PO Box 30314
Winston-Salem, NC 27130

First Edition

Cover design by Kevin Morgan Watson

Cover art, "Before the Spur" Copyright © 2010 by Dawn Cooper, used by permission of the artist.

Author photo by Dawn Cooper

Cover artist photo by Beverlee Cooper

Printed on acid-free paper
ISBN 978-1-941209-50-9

for Dawn,
bringer of balance

Acknowledgments

My thanks to the editors of the following magazines in which some of these poems first appeared:

Alabama Literary Review, "Bird as Metaphor for Bird"

Alaska Quarterly Review, "Total Balance Farm"

Dead Languages (Anhinga Press), "After the Honeymoon, Livestock," and "Brown Recluse"

Fifth Wednesday Journal, "Today's Lessons in the Animal Kingdom"

Gettysburg Review, "Sarah, Unbroken"

Tampa Review, "Waiting for the Next Ice Age" and "Ten Haiku About the Limitations of the Heart, with One Missing"

Great debts are owed to the following for inspiration and support: Dawn Cooper, Keith Ratzlaff, Jeff Gundy, Kevin Stein, David Wojahn, Jim Peterson, Tom Phillips, Emily Herring Wilson, Dean Young, and Kevin Watson.

Contents

Ball vs. the Afterlife

No pearls, no precious stones.
Just granite
from the abandoned quarry,
rough-cut and fissured.
Not much use at all.

Hope
is another embarrassment.
I'd do the impossible
if I could,
or at least the unlikely.
I'd call down
the hawk from the pine,
I'd explain the difference
between the darkness
of the cave
and the darkness
at the center of the sun.
I'd crowbar my speech
into a frame of mind that
hasn't been framed before.

But what can I say?
You know as much as I do.
We're equally unique,
equally as common as breath.
We see the same blue sky,
suffer, laugh,
long for the unreachable.
We've all plucked needles
from our hearts.
We've all seen the enemy smile.

So what if our parents were
chain-smoking alcoholics
wielding leather belts,
or whatever stark scene

your stunted childhood
might have been?
We're still around.
So what if there was damage?

My dog
is really my wife's dog,
though I named him.
He often looks worried.
If he's busy, he pretends
he doesn't hear my call.
But I control the word
that sets him whirling
by the door: *ball.*
Retrieving
is the only game he knows.
He'll cross most boundaries
for *ball.*

My life has no equivalent.
I never whirl,
except in secret.
My games are cold, rooted
in habit and arcane beliefs.
Schools have taught me
how to fetch,
but all my knowledge
has an expiration date.

I see my moments fade
into a lengthening line
of ghosts.

About the afterlife:
the rumor persists.
And why not?
We've known conception

and birth,
twin passages
that ended in surprise.
Who can say what's next?

Make your best guess
and call it religion,
that's how we operate,
some so afraid
of being wrong
they kill the doubters.

The Buddhists advocate
emptiness,
but what they mean is
don't buy that new car
or the big TV.
Right for the spirit,
wrong for the economy.
At least they understand
the kinship of opposites—
that yin and yang
are not divisible,
that the unseeing eye
and the all-seeing eye
are essentially the same.

There are things
I could say about
emptiness, but I won't,
which is a Zen approach.

By heritage I'm
Reformed Presbyterian,
which means I
no longer burn witches.
I married one, in fact,

when I was young:
a novice Wiccan
who stirred our
simmering cauldron
for two years, then wisely
put me on the street.
Another emptiness.

The sky starts with
emptiness,
that baseline blue,
but its nature is infinite,
always changing,
never the same sky twice.
That's why we keep watching,
even at night,
when stars give us reason
to wonder without ceasing.

Whether spurred by God
or dog, we chase things
in the mind—
that rented textbook
where every question
is a math problem at heart.
Check your worksheet
for examples:
Be fruitful and multiply
says the Black Book,
Divide and conquer,
says Julius Caesar,
Just add water,
says Betty Crocker.

And don't forget the writing
on the playground wall:
Billy + Suzy, Johnny + Jill,

all those seventh-grade
mysteries summed up by love,
equations held in balance
by a long line of irrational
and imaginary numbers.

Is each galaxy shaped
like a virus,
or is each virus
shaped like a galaxy?
The answer
always surprises me.

So what do we have besides
our loss of innocence,
of faith,
of self respect?
Even hope is a subset
of disappointment,
a wish
to retrieve something,
to regain that
rounded wholeness
in which we once believed.

Now there's a belief
for every decimal point in Pi.

And what is Pi?
An ironic, endless number-
the one we use to calculate
the volume of the ball.

A Note to My Daughters, Far Away

The heat of the afternoon
has eased into the gray haze
of evening; the oak tree,
with its broad city of leaves,
stands still
as the earth beneath it.

Time slows,
as it always does
for the solitary watcher.
Were I not here,
time might falter altogether.
As it is,
my faint shadow
in the fading light
will soon be gone.

O, my daughters:
for you I wish nothing
too steep,
too far,
too difficult to hold.

Given sad choices,
I would wish you doubt
before I would wish you pain.
I would wish you pain
before I would wish you
loneliness.

I would never wish you fear—
that inmost cave
where souls lose sight
of everything.
I've wandered there for
more eternities
than I can count,

yet still believe there is
a lighted pathway back.

Longing is unavoidable,
so live with it
as best you can.
Let it be an ally—
the hunger
that propels the hunt.

In every case, maintain
a celebration.
Remember some bright pool,
some dance
of light through leaves,
some spread of color
from a sinking sun.
The dark descends
only to remind us:
existence
was a long shot at best,
but luck was with us.
Let all complaints be feathers.

Hummingbird and Hawk

What surprises me most
about hummingbirds
is their viciousness.
We've hung feeders
on the back of the house,
and I've watched
from the kitchen window,
just inches away:
oil-slick greens and blues,
iridescent in the sun;
ruby throats on some.
A dozen or more might
swarm the red glass jars,
squabbling over the
false flower's fake nectar.
They'll drain a quart of
sugar water in a day.

A fragile, delicate bird—
the beak a slender thorn,
the body a mere
afterthought of creation.
The smallest can weigh
less than a penny.

But their recklessness
of attack, even when
food is plentiful,
suggests an inborn
state of panic,
a lack of judgment,
an incomplete understanding
of what a summer day
might bring.

Or maybe I'm the one
who doesn't understand.

Sometimes they rest
on the yellow rim
of the feeder's base,
appearing ordinary,
drab as a dwarf sparrow.

Flight is their comfort zone,
wings fanning faster
than the eye can see,
seventy beats per second.
All day long they fight,
bulleting through the yard,
beak to tail,
banking left and right,
each the interloper
to the other's
hunger and desire.

Nearby, our red-tailed hawk
sits solitary and calm
on the top rail at the
front end of the pasture.
He often perches
close to the horses—
their clumsy hooves will
sometimes flush out prey,
and he'll drop deftly
to the ground
for a field mouse no bigger
than a hummingbird.

He takes no notice of
the hummingbirds themselves,
those fidgety impersonators
that lack a raptor's knack
for ripping flesh from bone.

Hawk: even the word
lodges like a hatchet
in green wood.

Sometimes he rides
the high thermals,
seeing everything.

He once allowed me
to approach,
holding my stare
until he lost interest.
When I crowded too close,
just five steps away,
he noted my impertinence
by gliding a few rails
further down the line,
more dismissive than fearful.
No doubt he's seen
what humans can do,
but has nevertheless
pegged me as a weakling—
grounded, no stealth at all,
no speed, no patience,
my talons flimsy and dull.

Neither bird, I suspect,
shares my fondness
for rain on rusted tin,
sees faces in the clouds,
builds a logical argument,
leaves a proper tip.
The hawk cries out its presence
across the brambled fields,
the hummingbird
chirps petty objections.
Neither bird has a song.

Maybe that's
our common ground.

The hawk dwells
mostly in stillness,
in ownership.
The hummingbird flits,
a timid trespasser
in the hostile air,
its wild heart buzzing.

And yet they're both birds,
which means that somewhere
in the misty backstory of life
they shared a common ancestor,
some bird-like thing
that laid a clutch of eggs
of unequal size,
unequal possibility, and
the great divergence began.

Meanwhile,
I walk between the two,
imagining kinship
with both hummingbird
and hawk,
part of me believing
the nectar-filled world
has tumbled toward
a terrifying end,
part of me
believing it never will.

Sarah, Unbroken

My wife—Dawn—
a natural caretaker,
found a car-struck fawn
by the roadside
and brought it home,
a doubtful rescue
from the start.

She laid it in a stall
bedded with fresh sawdust
and set food and water
within its reach.

It never drank or fed.
Our soft voices
were no balm
for its broken back,
and nothing ever calmed
its panic into rest.

Nevertheless,
we named her,
that ancient human habit,
so prominent among
our weaknesses.

If need is great,
some animals surrender
to a soothing touch,
regardless of what
instinct has to say.
But others don't,
and this one clung to fear
as if it were her only hope.

She died
before the week was out,

the only ending possible,
and we grieved as if
we had an owner's right.

Maybe that was empathy,
or maybe just
the same old hubris,
left over from those
first free days in Eden,
when naming was
the only means we had
to stake a claim.

But either way,
she was never less
than wild,
and nothing about her
was ever really ours
except her name,
that artificial thread
of kinship and belonging,
an illusion
strung between ourselves
and the damage
we bring daily to the world.

Rejecting Lessons of the Fall

Day begins in silent gray,
dank, motionless,
on the cool cusp of autumn.
No birds chirp.
The horses stare
toward the highway as
morning stagnates
in the diffuse light.
A deep chill ignites
each supple branch.

Leaves begin their turn
in a multitude of signs,
as green becomes yellow,
then red, putting
a natural stop to things.

Across the bitten field
logging trucks drag
their flaking haul
toward whatever comes next.

Sooner or later the moon
will fall to earth,
but that's not our concern.

There's better news nearby:
the headwaters
of the great river start small,
shallow enough to wade across,
and that's how it is with
every problem in the world.

But fall is a biased teacher.
The maple and the elm uncloak
to show that every song
about life

is also a song about death.
The persimmon grows bitter,
and warns against
the evergreen optimism
of spruce and pine,
hemlock and cedar,
because the killing frost
is coming in, regardless.

But beware homilies
from the plant world.
Turn toward the light
sounds fine at first,
but we aren't daffodils.
How can we expose our backs
to darkness?

The days grow short,
and color drains away,
returning to the earth
through that irresistible
breakdown
we call decay.
If nature is the mirror,
what's our way out?
That's the question in the cold,
the one that haunts us
every circle of the sun.

We all struggle against
the armed camp of the psyche,
negotiating treaties
with each turn of the head,
each blink of an eye.
It isn't what we believe
that frightens us;
it's everything else.

In a spiral true
to the galaxy of our birth,
the world goes
down
and down
and we change nothing.

And that's okay.
One season calls up
curses from the dark,
but others
tell a different tale.
Open your eyes, they say.
The moon is still up there,
shining.

Total Balance Farm

What we can't say
is everywhere.

This morning
while the younger stallion
rolls in dust
to coat himself
against the flies,
I pull thistles from
the barbed-wire stretch
behind the pond.

The purple blooms look soft
and bright as childhood,
but sting
as deeply as the stalks.

Nothing friendly
grows in fence rows.

I duck with care
through the spotted shade
of the Osage orange—
hedge apple, we call it here—
its branches lined
with stunted spikes.

By afternoon I've moved on
to the tight weave of
buckthorn and briar that
curves across the floodplain

of the low front field.
Every fencepost leans rotten
against the slack
of unstrung wire.
I bake beneath the glare

of a clear sky, my arms
bloody with reprimands.

Back at the sheet-metal barn
a small frog clings
to a window pane.
A stork,
the first I've ever seen,
passes purposefully overhead.

The house waits quietly,
though five blue-backed
baby swallows clamor
from a nest above the porch.
The sun goes silver
behind its usual hill.
Moments gather,
possibly without end.

Still, what I can't say
is everywhere.

Dark is a narrow easement.
Dawn is a word I love.
Sometimes storms
wash through the valley,
and the cold stream
strays across the road.
But not today.

I scrape my boots clean
with a goat bone
left over
from the dogs' night out
and think which portions
of the widening earth
I'll try to move tomorrow.

Eagle and Turtle

When the eagle drops the turtle
from a great height,
it knows what it's doing.
That's how it makes a living.
The turtle will land hard,
preferably on rocks,
and split apart, allowing
easy access to the meat.

But what does the turtle
make of it all?
Falling from the sky
outstrips its understanding.
As far as any turtle knows,
gravity is harmless,
a slow pull toward lethargy,
a simple means of staying put.
Shell-shattering force
is a mystery of the afterlife,
a puzzle inherited by blood,
a secret text hidden among
the picked-over remains
of the fallen.

In that moment of release
does the turtle think
it's free
to get on with its life?
Is it pleased by
the weightless downward rush,
relieved
to have slipped the grip

of whatever it was
that snatched it up
from its sunny slant of stone
on the warm bank
beside the water?

Is the last thing it feels
a surge of joy
as it accelerates
headlong toward
what it has known only
as the safety of its home?

And what if it somehow lives,
landing lightly
on a cushion of thick brush,
or slicing edgewise
back into a mossy pond?

What facts of the miraculous
can it pass along
to others of its kind
when there are no others
of its kind?
Experience speaks a language
all its own.
Survivors are both
blessed and cursed,
and have to live alone
with what they know.

Who among the ordinary
could believe in
talons from the sky,
the terrifying rapture
of being taken up,
the ecstasy of flight,
the freedom of the great fall,
the shock of reuniting
with the rising earth?

Who among the innocent
could comprehend
the darkness

of the turtle's dream,
the one that now
casts its shadow
over all remaining
moments in the sun?

Crossing Braddock Run

On the far bank
      of Braddock Run
      in high summer
  you might find
  the deep satisfaction

primal
elemental
  of crossing quick water
  after a rain

It might not be easy

  Around your footing
nothing will lurk
but steady and
      irregular force

  the stones worn smooth
  and slippery
the shallow
      shattering
  surface of the run
  alive
  with imbalance
in the mottled
      morning light

Take a slow breath
  feel
the cool air
      of the shadows
  hear
the small water sounds
      rising

Look briefly back
then climb the rough bank

  if you can

and look closely
        at the heart
of the hydrangea's

pink flower
  blue flower
      white flower

Forget
  your life's obsession
with decay

Everything
      in the natural world
  is driven by beauty

We have much
     to live up to.

Elegy Against Elegies

The cold came hard,
as always,
shivering the trees bare.

I raked the leaves
and burned them.
Now, after three days,
I scoop the remnants
into plastic bags

and sweep
the oily residue away.
My hands are
stained with ash.

Once, in the same span
of days, my mother
died and was buried,
and each year I think
there must be something
I should do.

But my only ritual is
the rake,
the fire,
the broom.

There is no end
to earthly disappearances.
My father, too, is gone,
along with all my
elder kin.

My own children
look at me with
burdens beyond childhood
in their eyes.

When I depart
the world will
reinvent itself and
mysteries will multiply.

But that's not true.
The mundane
will hold steady.
Mail will pile up briefly
with my name.
People will busy themselves
against the fall
to no effect.
Time will be squandered
on the rake
the fire,
the broom.

After the Honeymoon, Livestock

The old routines
        soon disappear.

Today my wife
        milked a dead cow
        to save its newborn calf,
a white bull tangled
in ropy afterbirth.

She scissored the cold cord
        and hauled the bloody
        breathing mess
down the hillside to the barn,
        warmed it with a blanket.
        By afternoon it
stood steady on its own.

But later in the same field,
        as she worked the
unbroken stallion
        on a training line,
three jack burrows, stern
watchdogs of the cattle herd
        crested the hill
                and charged.

The spooked stallion whirled
                and trampled her
        then dragged her down
        the rocky slope.
A cracked sternum and more.

        As usual, she
        shrugged it off,
content to hold her balance
between misfortune
                and sheer grace.

In some worlds
the inexplicable always
        marries the inevitable,
             and we dance
like relatives from
        out of town,
        reeking of mothballs,
devouring
        the white cake afterwards.

Seeing vs. Believing

Extend a cane,
angled,
into a clear pool
and see
how the water lies.

A green streetlamp
casts
a reddish shadow
on the snow.

Horizon lines
waver
in summer heat,
liquid as light.

A ghost appears,
then vanishes,
in the corner
of an eye.

Little is what
or where
it claims to be.

Nothing is honest,
save
the ordinary
question mark,

a curve in space
amid a world
of straight
deceptions,

a symbol

severed
from its lower
self,

a clear sign
of wonder,

an endless voice
with no pretense
of knowing.

Contemplating Wilderness at 30,000 Feet

Progress
might be too optimistic
a word
for what we're making.

When wilderness
was status quo,
grim pilgrims
stood their ground.

We're soft as
rain-soaked grass.
We spend our lives
in track shoes, shifting
on hot pavement,
cold pavement,
buckled pavement.
We stroll the malls.
Between vacations
we calibrate machines
to put up walls
between nature and
our well-dressed selves.

But time disrupts
even as it levels,
and I'm the outlier
on the ragged edge,
settled in against the
rough back of the woods.

I hammer fence boards,
hack away at stumps,
stack hay in storage sheds.
I rake the stalls and
haul manure to the fields.

But something watches
from a hidden perch.
Cougars have
marked our woodlands,
our pastures, as their own.

A young one
crossed our road at dusk:
the tail long,
the body sleek and low.
At night we hear the squall,
like an infant
crying to be fed.

The lame horse
in the near paddock
spooks at nightfall,
frantic for the barn.
The dogs bark
at what's unseen.

Everything that lives here
qualifies as prey,
even the well-educated,
and somewhere
in that common blackness
is a thing that
can't be reasoned with.
It's ready,
should the stumble come.

We still walk out
on moonless nights
for necessary chores,
a tuned ear turned always
toward the brush.
I keep a pitchfork

by the riding ring
and scan the trees for eyes.

Tonight I'm traveling,
safe among strangers,
cruising the blank sky
at an altitude no animal
could dream.

Even this is wilderness,
and nature's lesson
is the same:
all flights are temporary.
We might delay, delay,
and then delay again,
but the cat
is down there waiting,
its mind clear,
its need growing with
each passing winter's day.

Fevers of the Bodies

Last week snow,
now this warm spell.
Flies have taken over
the tack room,
a first for February.

Call it global warming.
Call it polar vortex.
Call it anything.
Naming is akin to owning,
and owning grants
illusions of control.

These days I tire quickly,
so far without dying,
but we all know
that won't last.

At the clinic they name
ailments common
to my demographic,
but my night terrors
have them stumped.
A side-effect, maybe,
of some helpful pill.

The woman I love
has ten dark symptoms
of her own, but doctors
won't confirm a diagnosis.
That disappoints;
we're a labeling species.
How do we diminish
what can't be named?

God understood
that problem, that threat,

and dodged it for a while.
But language
triumphed in the end
and shrunk omnipotence
down to three
small letters and a name.

I guess there's nothing
we won't do
to get a handle on things.

Meanwhile, back at the ranch,
we both pretend the sun
comes up the same.
We feed the animals,
clear manure from the fields,
and sit long hours
where the sun streaks in
between the blinds.

At night
I watch the sky for fire.
I take a shallow breath
and hold it.

Waiting for the Next Ice Age

Coach said,
If you can't play hurt,
you can't play.
Turns out he was right.

I have friends
with broken heads and
different hearts
and all those secret,
silent ailments of the blood.

But I've learned a few things.
The universe is a war
between curves and angles.
Bugs fly toward the light
that kills them. Saturdays
aren't what they used to be.
A scattering of nails
outside a tire store
is cause for suspicion.

I try smiling, but the mirror
is a growing disappointment.

True reflection
is me at seventeen,
cornering hard
with the top down,
the wind still welcome,
the road
more slippery than I thought.

Today's Lessons in the Animal Kingdom

The horses need more room
to run, so I'm pulling
fence posts that divide
the larger field.

It's late July, heat
shimmers from the yellow dirt,
and I pace myself,
digging a while, sorting
old boards, digging again.

I guess correctly
as I turn the knotted planks,
expecting black widows
before finding them.
We're infested here.

I step with purpose
on the largest one,
but when I lift my boot
she's gone.
I pick my shovel up again.

The job takes longer
than I thought it would,
as most jobs do.
Each inch is earned,
so tight and sure
the stonelike grip of earth.

The horses watch my progress
from a farther field,
flinching against deer flies,
patient in the sun.

The dog watches from the porch,
too wise to leave the shade.

Were I his equal,
I'd have no posts to pull,
no tools to work
the reclaimed land.
I'd hold no obligation here,
feel no owner's urge
to measure and confine.

As it is, I'm tethered
to these few acres,
a minor stop on Lee's
retreat toward Appomattox.
Spent bullets from the war
undercoat the territory,
but true history
carves a broader trail.

Here's what solid ground
has taught me:
there is no solid ground.
Each fence row is a fluid thing,
no matter how deep
the posts are set.
The straight line I etched
across the field last year
broke ranks in early spring.

The soil loosened and shifted,
erasing all my efforts
at precision and control,
then hardened into place again.

That's natural enough.
The earth breathes upheaval,
making and unmaking mountains
with a shrug.
Around here, weeds and vines

handle the small stuff,
dismantling whatever board
or brickwork we devise.

The dog offers a lethargic yawn,
and I suspect he's right.
Our deeds are made of paper.
The rest is made of clay.

Bird as Metaphor for Bird

1.

the space we know
is finite: wings

are more for consolation
than escape

even in flight
a bird is tethered

2.

a winter portrait of
fifty black vultures
in a sycamore tree
moves no one

but a portrait of
destruction
fires the mind

hunters flush a pheasant
from the field
and bring it down

feelings vary
by circumstance:
joy for the hungry
sorrow for the empathetic
pleasure for the
damaged or inadequate
something else
for the rest

meaning ought to fit in
somewhere

preserve the single bird
blasted from the sky

open a place in memory
for whatever
abstract notion
captures its fall.

The History of Religion

A man stares too long
at the sun
then falls in love
with what he thinks
he sees.
He raves, naturally.

Listeners gather,
mistaking blindness
for insight's
nearest kin.

A shred of wet
cardboard streaked
with oil and rust from
the broken-bricked
alley floor

becomes

a long, bright room,
a flock of doves,
a circus of acrobats
and mysterious beasts
on the edge
of a golden city.

Someone sends 'round
the collection plate.
Belief will side
with what's pretty.

Leftover Wishes

I wanted to be a cowboy
    like my grandfather

become that lean horseman
    standing in front
    of the cigar store
near the railway depot

  twirling a rope, a lariat,
no chaps because
    they look stupid
  but yes, a pair of jangly spurs
    on well-stitched boots

a silver buckle balancing
  a sixgun slung low
    both glinting in the sun

    certainly a hat
    dusty white
not ten gallon, but smaller
  with a sharp crease
    and a curved brim
    more Colorado than Texas

my palomino idling
    by the hitching post
  flicking flies with his tail

nowhere special to go
  nowhere special
    I haven't already been

dust in the street
a dollar in my pocket

    that's all, that simple

       but
between my first ambition
and my last

  wind comes howling
down the arroyos
kicking up dust and
  reshaping the territory

something rattles
                 something strikes
        and suddenly cowboys
aren't
       what they used to be

the cutting horse
       dissects the herd

  life gets complicated.

Trash

Sunday evenings at the dump
I toss whatever's
broken or irrelevant.

It's never easy.
No one wants to call a thing
unsalvageable.

But what good is a
splintered axe handle,
a rotted ladder,
a cracked bucket?

Why save machine parts
after the machines are gone,
or stacks of roofing shingles,
thick with moss and mold,
or sacks of concrete
hardened into stone?

Forget history,
that cesspool
of nostalgia and regret.
The world says usefulness
is a here-and-now affair,
the opposite
of what's eternal.
Worn out is a death sentence
even for the faithful,
and *pointless*
is the point of no return.

I like the ride home,
the truck bed empty,
my life free of waste.

But in the rearview mirror
I see what lies ahead:
everything thought,
everything written,
everything that once
blazed brightly or amazed.

Just after the last fork,
even the highway
turns to dust.

Brown Recluse

Because her boots have stood
too long in the tack room,
she turns them over
and gives them a good shake—
enough to coax a pebble loose,
but not a web.

Her mind has leapt ahead—
the new barn needs
its coat of yellow paint
before the mold sets in,
and first she has to work the
younger gelding in the killing heat.

Each day serves up a hardship,
but a blessing, too,
and though it's crossed her mind
to hesitate, she can't resist
the forward plunge that takes her
to a world she loves,
the wild horse learning signs
beneath her, her black boots
shining in the sun.

When the Teacher Is Ready
the Student Will Appear

At the big university
there's a
No Trespassing sign
on the School
of World Studies.

Nearby, mathematicians
don't notice;
they're busy
summing up the problem.

Across campus
among the philosophers
Socrates
goes on screaming
Know thyself, you
stupid sons of bitches!

but the sound
doesn't carry
quite far enough.

Ten Haiku About
the Limitations of the
Heart, with One Missing

The mirror reflects
the face that reflects the world
that holds the mirror.

Light brightens any
space, but that's illusion. There
are still bills to pay.

We wait for someone
to appear, but the heart has
four clouded windows.

Every storm kills some
thing, but keep smiling: nothing
distracts like rainbows.

Dance and the heart will
thaw; thaw and the heart will dance.
But mind the music.

The empty street and
the crowded street are the same:
strangers remain strange.

Language is the mask
concealing our uneven
heartbeats from the world.

In pure wilderness
the only clear path is the
one right behind you.

So in the smallest
of rooms, which is to say the
heart, we rest at last.

Personal Inventory

Things I never developed a taste for:
caviar, the lottery, revenge, hockey,
German Expressionism, piano lessons,
long distance running, Wyoming, opera,
hot peppers, and certain kinds of death.

Things I slowly developed a taste for:
artichokes, cemeteries, geometry,
speed limits, a chilly dawn,
a long straight fence row, ear muffs,
and unidentifiable noises in the woods.

Things I once had a taste for, but
got over: berber carpeting, hamsters,
bean-bag chairs, large cardboard boxes,
roller coasters, climbable trees, muddy
hillsides, off-off-Broadway, and mime.

Things I've always been okay with:
cats, gyroscopes, primary colors,
the smell of a chlorinated pool,
the whine of trucks on the highway,
fiber optics, hoofbeats on hard
ground, xylophones, and hats.

Things about which I'm undecided:
the quadratic equation, mules,
pomegranates, bicycles with more than
three speeds, the infinite smallness
of subatomic space, the endless
emptiness beyond the last star, and
the remaining mystery of everything.

Traveling Before the Dark

after William Stafford

You've heard about the deer, about how Bill
had to stop and roll the damn thing off the
dark road to keep everybody safe. Well,
I'm the careless ass who hit it. And yeah,

I left the bloated carcass there for him
to deal with, so I guess that makes me the
bad guy here. What do you want me to say?
Am I supposed to whine about my day,

my divorce, cutbacks at the plant, bad debts?
That's just life, no special drama to it.
My mind was elsewhere, that's all, and when I
crested that last rise, I shut my eyes

against the glare. Anybody would. And
okay, maybe I had a weak moment.
But don't pretend you don't know what it's like—
that darkness when temptation beats inside

you like a second heart. I imagined
swerving, that long freefall to the river.

The *impact* is what kept me on the road.

The Loss of Horses

Understanding is a threshold
to be broken twice:
the wrong idea
followed by the right.

Wrong
is often more agreeable.

When I first heard the word
I felt confusion,
then delight: *melancholy*
on a child's blank slate,
carries no darkness.
Instead, a form impossible
for the wise to see
assembles itself
in the unworldly mind.

I pictured a dog,
part melon, part collie.
A shiny green body,
four legs of twining vines,
a wagging stem of a tail,
a leafy tongue lolling
from a mouth that smiled.
My melancholy dog was happy.

And why not?
Nothing in an untried world
requires a sombre mood.
Innocence is an empty state,
a yardstick

by which we measure loss,
so I was busy
cataloguing data:
water was wet,
rocks were hard,

heat was hot,
pain was painful.
Being new here
was a full-time job.

I knew by then what
horses were.
Sometimes they carried cowboys
across the grassy plain.
Sometimes they hauled
storybook gods across the sky.
Only later
would I sort the differences,
distinguish mind from body,
separate the mythic
from the real.

After breathing,
misinformation
is the first high hurdle
of childhood.

After breathing,
misinformation
is the first safe haven
of childhood.

But when our fun
with Dick and Jane is done,
after we've seen Spot run,
disillusionment
dog-ears every page.
Horseflies
turn out not to be
the fairyland wonder
we first thought.
They're bloodsuckers,
always on the attack.

On the educated side of life,
discoveries are rare.
I find there's not much meat
on a chicken wing,
and when a kid yells,
Look at me, I'm a monkey,
the broken arm comes next.
Crestfallen
is our loveliest word
for disappointment.

For twelve years I've
lived with horses
that do not fly.
My wife repairs the ones
in need, and so I've learned
of all the fatal options:
torn tendons, colic,
bloody abscesses, laminitis,
ataxia, infectious anemia,
West Nile Virus, acidosis,
protozoal myeloencephalitis,
Cushing's Syndrome,
the strangles,
perforated coffin bones,
brain fever,
broken vertebrae, and
the inability to sweat.

We had an Irish sport horse
that ran a splintered
fence board through its skull.

Fragile in so many ways.

But sometimes indestructible.
When a neighbor's horse
got hit by a truck

on the highway,
my wife plunged her arm
inside its opened chest and
gripped the torn artery shut
until the vet arrived.
That horse survived.

It's all a mystery.
We've put down strong spirits
that foundered
for no clear reason,
and mad spirits,
and gentle spirits.
The best, called Beau,
is buried in our yard
between a thriving birch
and a dying magnolia.

Now, as the world shrinks
with age, we're scaling back
and giving up the farm.
No more rumbling stutter
of hoofbeats across
dusty ground at feeding time,
or the sharp swish of a tail
in the smoldering stillness
of a summer noon.

Our heroes once were cast
as bold equestrians
in bronze or stone.
Today the horse stumbles,
obsolete
as the gods themselves,
replaced by tractors
on the farm, cars
on the byways;
reduced to lawn ornaments,

or showpieces
for games the rich still play.
Bred for speed and thus
unnaturally frail,
the finest stallion
can snap a leg bone
before three-quarters of a mile.
The horse's day is done.

And yet we've found no
substitute in our mythology.
No one sculpts
Churchill atop a Volkswagen,
Eisenhower grinning
from his golf cart,
seven-iron in hand.
No one chisels Gandhi
riding the roller coaster,
or Mother Theresa
skimming the waves
on a jet ski,
a surge of horsepower
keeping her afloat.

Our statuary has shriveled
into life-sized likenesses
of unassuming souls
at ease in business suits,
pausing on a morning's walk,
often with a cane.
No sword held high,
no armored breastplate,
no rearing steed.
At most, a pensive look ahead.

On the placid lawn outside
the administration building,
a bronze man sits posed

on a park bench, resting,
as if metal fatigue
has already set in, as if
he's tired of celebrating
his own mild heroism,
wearied by the glory
of who he was.

Our very dreams, it seems,
have been diminished
by the exit of the horse,
and I'm awash in what
the ancients called
black bile,
dark product
of the gall bladder,
marked by foul humors
and a lengthening
of depressive dread.

The word they coined
for such a state,
I since have learned,
is *melancholy*.

Birthright

When we arrive, pained and
baffled, all speech is mystery.

Sure, we have some basic
answers in our blood, our

bones, whatever DNA provides.
We breathe without thinking.

We generate a pulse; consume,
digest, expel. We sweat.

Cleave is our first instinct,
and since the mind has not yet

learned to interfere we
know when to bind and when

to sever. Then words take
shape, for ball, for door.

We cry the wish to be lifted
up, the wish to be fed, the

wish to be comforted. Shades
of meaning cheat us out of

certainty, and stutter the heart
with vague directions home.

Only after years of dying in
cold alleys can we know that

life is not a thing to be
conquered, or even put into

words. Birth is a passage
we won't remember, and so is

death, but the middle is what
matters. We're more than just

prisoners waiting to be let
out. We are the universe

asking itself a question.
We are the part that wonders.

Call to Worship

The old church three farms
down the road burned to

the ground. Now it's a
charred scar on a small

rise, nothing left of it but
history and a homeless

congregation. But someone
will donate a scraggly plot

a few miles up the highway,
and they'll rebuild.

It's what we all do when
day capsizes into night,

when the whirlwind comes,
or the flood, or in this

case, lightning. Even so,
buildings don't matter in

the end. The body is a
stain upon the soul, or so

they say, and at times I
see the logic. Nature

drives a one-sided bargain,
and it's tough to know

where we fit in. Deer and
deer ticks flourish as

much as possum or raccoon,
but we're out of step,

killing on impulse, like
the lone cat or, worse,

the pack-bound dog.
At Total Balance Farm

the horses come and go,
the hawk watches, the

weather changes. Cobwebs,
coated in stall dust,

hang like silk stockings
from the barn rafters.

The riding ring offers up
sea shells after a rain,

the remnants of an ancient
time. I wish I could say

what life is like in
this place of shelter

and sudden dangers, but
language fails to measure

up, even to the ordinary.
The more a word is used,

the less it means, so some
things we take on faith,

like displaced congregants
continuing the habit of

prayer. Any piece of land
is holy if we name it so.

You think seeing is believing?
Humans know the moon has

no light of its own. But
it still beats the darkness.

Questions for the Long Flight Home

The City of Angels has been kind,
a scrapbook glimpse
of possibility, of wearied,
hopeful faces shining
through the glittered grime,
a child's idea of grandeur,
the Queen Mary moored nearby,
the tar pits fenced
and fitted with a gift shop
selling plastic bones.
The palms, the scraggly hills,
the red clay roofs.
Music drizzling through
second-rate speakers in
hole-in-the-wall cafes.
The old hotel that housed
the drunk inhabitants of Oz.
I've walked in sunlight here.

In Hollywood a small-town boy
might take on all comers and win—
though winning is relative.
Every top dog dies,
quietly, out of sight,
somewhere beyond the lobby.
The rest of us carry on,
salvaging our unscripted,
unfilmed lives.
The most we can earn is
respite, a few easy breaths.

The universe has no idea
which way is up,
but the brain does,
and that's our limitation.
We say the sun comes up,
but it doesn't.

We say that time is up.
But is it?

Is questioning a proper way
to pass the time,
stalling before take-off,
waiting for the next door
to open, the next engine
to spark back into life?

Is life
a victory tour
for beating the odds?

Or is life just a way
for the universe
to brag about itself?

Up can be another word for *out*,
and that's where we're headed,
all of us,
even the universe itself,
expanding, as it does,
more deeply into dark.
The circle always widens,
and that's why Pi is infinite,
that's why there's always
room to move around.
Is that our source
of limitless uncertainty?

Swans are not common in my life,
but ugly ducklings
quack incessantly,
as every teacher knows.
Is that our source of hope?

Technology started as a shortcut,
but sidewalks,
hallways,
aisleways
are more disorganized than ever.
Young walkers stare down
at glowing screens.
Rude encounters multiply.

The woman waiting for her plane
lied about the seat beside her,
saving it only for her carry-on.
I might wish her a rough flight,
but it's my flight, too.

Is jet-lag
our ordinary state,
stuck as we are
on the spinning world?
Do time zones bring
confusion to the blood?

Pythagoras believed in harmony
among all movements
in the sky, calling it
the Music of the Spheres.
Today air traffic
is our main concern.
Is that what we mean by progress?

In my own small version
of the grand scheme of things,
the Big Bang is less intriguing
than the Small Awakening,
that first bearing of witness
when something blinked
and looked around.
Color, shape, movement—

nothing can be real without
perception to proclaim it,
to provide the word that
pins the butterfly to its board.
Without the eye,
the universe goes unobserved,
its fires and misfires unrecorded.
Subtract the mind,
and reality empties out,
becoming less than imaginary.
What's less than the imaginary?

My questions are all rhetorical,
which is to say unanswerable,
which is to say nothing.

When I was a small boy my wish
was to grow big enough
to do what I wanted.
Does anyone ever get that big?

Turbulence is a reminder
of how out of place we are.
But so are floods, earthquakes,
whirlwinds, lightning.
Is there such a thing
as solid ground?

Where is the line between
what's right
and what's left?

Is longing
the only message in the song?

Through a glass, darkly,
we watch idiots on parade,
then someone gets elected.

We learn words
like focus and perspective,
but the eyes don't always see.
Is depth perception
the first truth
or the first illusion?

At some point we made a choice
between cows that stand in fields
and cows that jump the moon,
and that determined all the rest.

This altitude brings
thoughts of God.
But what doesn't?
It's how I was raised.
When the highway claimed my dog,
I held his dead weight close
and watched his eyes grow fixed,
me not knowing what to offer,
neither of us
knowing what to expect.

What won't there be in heaven?
Accidents? Loss? Anger?
Styrofoam? Bathrooms?
A difference of opinion?
Talking for eternity
about how nice things are
is one of many hells.
Can I sing there
if I can't sing here?
Who will I sound like,
if not myself?
Who will listen to me sing?

Will there be nap time?
What dreams can be dreamed?

Or is heaven an ill-conceived
promise, an idea that nobody
ever really thought through?

Is heaven just a cheerful word
for dead?

I'm here on high
where prophets thought the
architect worked mainly
in motifs of pearls and gold.
There's nothing out the window
but a floor of clouds.

Maybe what they overlooked
was life itself: true heaven.
The paradise of present tense.

Because we're civilized,
we prefer crickets to roaches,
charmed as we are
by their chirping, leaping legs.
We prefer bees to spiders
though bees are more often deadly.
Is honey that important?

My conscience is no cricket.
It's a spider centered in a web
spun wide in all directions.
Every tremor draws it forward,
fangs bared, eager
to feed on my entanglements.

Has the anhinga lifted
its long legs
from the swamp and flown away?

I sit between a woman sleeping
and a woman translating Sanskrit.
Which is more
separated from the world?

Questions
for the martyred saints:
1. Why did you do that?
2. Any regrets?

More questions
for the martyred saints:
1. Hello?
2. Anybody there?

What title suits
the story of our lives?
What story suits the soul?
What soul deserves distinction?

Or is the best soul
the least distinct,
the least experienced,
the least distinguishable
from the great oneness?

Yet the well-worn shoe
fits better on the foot.
Maybe all I need
is a little polish,
a good shine to get me
through the door.

The seatbelt sign
reminds us there are
speed bumps in the sky.
Air currents can be as
solid as anything else,

and we never see them coming.
A baby in the next row
squawks demands
in a language only he knows.
Or maybe they aren't demands,
maybe they're questions
from a soul so fresh it
wonders what it's doing
back in the sky already,
soaring so close to the sun.

The cabin lights go down
and I see that
in following the earth's curve
we have left the sun behind.

Why do seats have to be in the
upright position before landing?
Will an upright position save me
if calamity strikes?
Most preachers think so.

Descent begins before we feel it.
I'll be careful when opening
the overhead bins.
Some contents may have shifted.

My talent, like the talent
of this riveted machine,
lies in motion, not in song.
I can juggle, but not whistle.
I can strike a ball,
but singing is beyond
my earthly reach.
Math problems are the closest
I can come to making music.
Thinking is the only voice I own.

Still, every limitation
offers hope.
I nestle down in this hammock
hung between stasis and flight
and silently compose myself.

I hear a strained rhythm
in the unwinding of gears,
the unfolding of wheels.
People around me speak the last
of what they have to say
before we finally touch down.

I listen for the melody
in every string of words
and try to take notes.

Sky was the first mystery,
the first music,
and as we throttle back
just enough to fall
unfatally to the ground,
I try to make something
of it all:
an understanding
broad enough to orchestrate
meaning in a
sometimes meaningless life.

But nothing sticks.
The Eternal survives
everything
except an explanation.

Music and mystery
are all we'll ever know.

The Repetition of Simple Words

I'll start with a fact:
Billy Faught died in a war.

That Billy's last name was Faught
is something too heavy-handed for fiction,
where the author gets to make such choices.
But I have no choice here.
Billy's last name was Faught.

There's no interesting or exciting story
about the Viet Cong firing on his helicopter.
The report offers no vivid sensory details to
make the experience of his death come alive.
I can't say what happened
because I wasn't there.

But here are some details that survive,
paltry as they are,
some from the official record,
some from what I know:

Billy was a year and five months older,
but we were in the same draft lottery—
the first since World War II—
and boys of both our ages
were being swept up.
His number was 117, mine was 122,
and that was the slim difference between us.

Maybe he enlisted when his number hit,
hoping to improve his odds
of landing a plum assignment.
Or maybe he waited until they called him up
and just let the chips fall.
Maybe he'd have joined anyway,
whatever his number,
for pure love of country.
I don't know.

Was he anxious? Excited? Fatalistic?
I have no idea.
Whatever his circumstance,
he began his tour of duty on
May 26th, 1970, when he was nineteen.

I was eighteen, finishing high school,
having the time of my life.
My draft number was borderline,
but I kept my fingers crossed.
Things looked good for my deferment:
I'd been accepted into college.
My girlfriend was a blond cheerleader
who said she'd marry me
if I got sent to Viet Nam.

I don't know if Billy had a girlfriend.

My great-aunt may have told me once
that Billy had a pregnant wife,
but I'm not sure, time having left
so many thick clouds on the horizon.
But that would explain a lot.
With a family to support,
he'd have likely dropped out of school,
and Selective Service always
moved in fast on boys like that.
But I don't know.
Maybe there was no wife, no child.
Maybe there was no one.

Billy snagged a job
that should have kept him safe:
helicopter mechanic.
Not part of the crew,
just someone who repaired problems
back at the base.

The date of his *incident*—
which is the term the Army uses—
was July 25th, 1970, just two months in.
I was probably playing golf,
going to the movies, having fun.
It was my last summer
before leaving home.

Specialist Fourth Class Billy Faught
died in Bien Hoa Province,
and his body was recovered.
His *casualty type*—
another term the Army uses—
was *non-hostile*.
Non-hostile, it reads.
Died of other causes.

Further down the form,
under *casualty detail*,
there's no detail at all,
just a category:
air loss over land.

In four subsequent categories,
the designations read:
was not MIA
was not MIA
was not MIA
was not MIA
Simple words repeated
like a grade-school primer.

To most people Arlington, Virginia,
means the cemetery
where so many of our soldiers rest.
But Billy had a native claim
on Arlington. He was born there.

He grew up there. He could see
the Washington Monument from his yard.

Here's one possibility:
Billy was working on the ground
when a damaged helicopter,
struggling to make it back to base,
fell on him from the sky.

Here's another possibility:
Billy took a ride
in a damaged helicopter
to assess repairs.
It fell with him inside.

I prefer the second version,
the one that, for a brief time,
lifts Billy up.

The first version curses me:
I can see Billy chopped apart
by helicopter blades
as he tries to run for cover.
Now I've burdened you with that image,
even though I can tell you plainly
it's pure imagination.
I don't know what happened.
I wasn't there.
I've never been there.

But there are places I've been,
places all over the country,
all over the world.
One of those places,
one of the most important,
was Arlington, Virginia, when I was five.
Billy lived in the building next door
and had already started first grade.

There's not much I can say about the boy.
He was bigger than I was, of course,
but his size was normal for his age.
I think he had brown hair.
I know that he was nice.
I know that for the two years I was there
he stuck by me, a solid pal.

I told him I was afraid to go to school
because I couldn't read—
and from what I understood,
reading was something that went on there.
So Billy said he'd teach me how,
and every day we huddled over the pages
of his book—*Fun With Dick and Jane*—
as he moved his fingers over the letters,
sounding out the simple repetition of
simple words until I knew enough
to say them for myself.

Billy opened a door,
and I passed through into a world
of Dick and Jane,
Baby Sally and their dog, Spot.
There may have been a cat named Puff,
though memory across so many years
allows me little certainly.

In any case, through Billy's heart
I learned to read, and since that time
I've read a hundred thousand tales.
That's more than Milton ever read,
and more than Shakespeare.
Nothing special about it, though—
we're in an age of access.
We can read anything we think to look for.

So here I am.
My lengthening trail of words
has circled back and brought me
to a place I never wished to be:
Billy's own last page,
a bureaucratic log
on a government web site,
a bundle of bare facts
fastened to a name
carved on the Memorial Wall:
Panel 8, Line 51:
William Avener Faught, Jr.

Some facts, of course, go unrecorded.
Our favorite page showed Dick
sailing his toy plane on the wind.
It soared away from him into a blue sky
while Jane and Sally watched in awe.
Up, up, said Baby Sally. *Go up, up, up.*

The Inevitability of Last Words

When something unnatural burns,
the smell can't help but bring suspicion:
acrid smoke might mean the worst.

Normally, I'd worry, but not this time.
Neighbors cackle out conversation
across the road, and a diversity of birds

chatters unalarmed above the weedy,
hard-baked ground. Unlooked for, a
memory shivers loose from the trees,

shrugging off the weight of more than
half a century, and suddenly I'm back
where I started, in a time when other

birds chirped, a blue breeze shifted, and
that same stink drifted in from the fire pit
out back, where castoffs of our daily life

were fed to flames, their forms darkening
from every bright color into ash, harmless,
we believed, as the dusty light slanting

through the living room. I can feel the
bristled rug beneath my knees, see
my grandmother's marble-topped tables,

ashtrays everywhere, a wind-up clock
on the granite mantle above the
granite hearth, roses on the wallpaper,

my parents smiling their happy-family
smiles from the crackling plastic of
the couch, still immune to life's most

catastrophic ends. Cicadas beyond
the black screen door whir through
the sluggish afternoon, and my

great-grandfather blesses us at
dinnertime with his mumbled prayer,
then beats me at checkers afterwards.

They all had some last thing to say,
I guess, but nothing stuck. Now I'm
their only trace. Gradually, I've slipped

inside the stitching of lost ancestors,
layering them over me like hand-me-
down clothes. What here is solely mine?

Or am I just a bulk inheritance of genes,
the pieces of my puzzle jigsawed from
bygone versions of myself? Our self.

When I bend to watch a praying mantis
scale a stalk of golden rye, am I the
prehistoric one? The medieval one?

The one who doctored Andrew Jackson
in the sad war against the Creeks?
The one who lost his printing press

to General Sherman on his march?
The one whose honeymoon ended in the
great San Francisco earthquake and fire?

More likely, I'm the multitudes I'll never
know—farmers, firemen, horse thieves,
midwives, preachers, beggars, kings.

They linger in the way my hand grips
an axe, a spoon, a steering wheel;
in the way my brow furrows at a leaky

roof or limbs creaking in a gale. They
linger in my fear of dark alleys, my hatred
of the cold, my taste for turnip greens.

More and more my answer to the dead
is: *Oh. I see.* My answer to the rest of
us is silence, awkward and tomblike.

My father, who flew bombing runs
in World War II, once told me he had
heard a pilot's final words: *Uh-oh,*

the boy had said, and that's about as
universal as it gets. In the end, we all
want to do our family proud, we all want

to spend that last breath blurting some
brilliant p.s. they'll be quoting in the high
schools. Who wouldn't want to cry out

something never said before, something
that identifies the rank genesis of all our
longing? But let's face it, some things

are easier done than said. I do believe it's
out there, the answer to the unarticulated
mystery, written into everything we know—

earth, air, water, fire, time's most antique
alphabet. But knowledge is a labyrinth
with no exit strategy. Who can read signs

in the garden at midnight? Who can stand
before the blank chalkboard and explain
things to the class? At odd times, alone

beside a mailbox, or in a car, or even
in a dream, I feel as if I've come within
arm's length of the unnamable, believe

myself balanced on the verge of
comprehending that the white stone is
not just the white stone, but is also the

scuffed root arching above the broken
earth, the brittle veins of last year's leaf,
the ant racing along the porch boards,

the vanished wind catching its own
breath, the burst of flowers—yellow,
purple, red—in the greening corner pot,

the solid shape of everything around me,
the thoughts that even now ignite new
brushfires in the dry wilds of my brain.

Friend, when I'm done with oxygen and
blood, speechless, not another word
to my name, please do me the kindness

of assuming I was finally there, lounging
at the nexus, when death stepped in; that
the material and the immaterial coalesced;

that diamonds dissipated into pure ideas
while pure ideas became diamonds.
But don't oversell it; don't say that

someone seeded the clouds with angels
and the sky rained proverbs without
number; don't say that language

geysered up from the dark, flooding the
earth with light, spilling all secrets,
washing all questions away. I may go

quietly, or not; singing, raving, or flinging
vile curses at the nurse. So forget last
words. It's enough if what I find upon

leaving is a fresh start, or at least a
fresh perspective, or even just one split
second free of all loneliness and regret.

A green field, a yellow sun, a rabbit in the
morning brush, a baseball nestled in a glove;
anything but the nothing of a black sky. Give

me anything, and I'll call it a fair exchange,
equal in value to all the time I spent wondering
in this charred and ever-changing land.

Clint McCown has published four novels (*The Member-Guest, War Memorials, The Weatherman*, and *Haints*), and four previous volumes of poems (*Labyrinthiad, Sidetracks, Wind Over Water*, and *Dead Languages*). He has received the Midwest Book Award, the Society of Midland Authors Award, the S. Mariella Gable Prize, the Germaine Breé Book Award, an Academy of American Poets Prize, a Barnes & Noble Discover Great New Writers designation, and a Distinction in Literature citation from the Wisconsin Library Association. He is the only two-time recipient of the American Fiction Prize. In journalism, he received an Associated Press Award for Documentary Excellence for his investigations of organized crime. He has worked as a screenwriter for Warner Bros. and a Creative Consultant for HBO television. He is a former principal actor with the National Shakespeare Company, and several of his plays have been produced. He has edited a number of literary journals, including the *Beloit Fiction Journal*, which he founded in 1984. He teaches in the MFA program at Virginia Commonwealth University and in the low-residency MFA program at the Vermont College of Fine Arts.

Dawn Cooper has been working with photography of animals and landscapes for decades. With an excess of 30 years specializing in animal training and rehabilitation, she launched her holistic classes utilizing photography to instruct owners and professionals of dogs and horses on therapeutic rehabilitation. Learn more at www.totalbalancemethod.com

CPSIA information can be obtained
at www.ICGtesting.com
Printed in the USA
BVOW03s2159130617
486839BV00001B/27/P